Celestia

A collection of poems by

Anisha Gupta

Celestia

A collection of poems by

Anisha Gupta

PAPER TOWNS
PUBLISHERS

PAPER TOWNS
PUBLISHERS

First published by
Papertowns Publishers
72, Vishwanath Dham Colony,
Niwaru Road, Jhotwara,
Jaipur, 302012

Celestia

ISBN Print Book – 978-93-94670-28-0

Cover by Neha Agrawal
nehaa.2089@gmail.com

I dedicate this book to my mother,
who is a quill in my life,
writing my story on every page of her heart.
She gave words to my character,
the day when I was born
to speak poetry.

Vinny Jain

Contents

I am my beloved

Solo

A new ray of hope, a refreshing wave of euphoria comes
As I soar into the sky, with wounds that are sore.
High as a free bird,
I came from a caged home,
Of dark and gloomy secrets.
The devil of hundred sins,
Was spouse to my angelic soul.
The "soulmate" in me longed to fly solo,
Of leaving the hells, and ringing the bells
Of heavenly skies.
The deep waters that hold,
medicine to cure my wounds.
The scorching sun that holds,
Warmth to give to my cold soul.
Let me lay in the million fragments,
Of the victory, that's sand.
As I stand before you,
Waving my white flag,
After battling through tough storms.
Let me have the taste,
Of the food in my basket,
And let me savour,
The juicy flavour,
Of having it in calm and clear space.
After all the rage and rush,
Comes the soothing hush.

Of enlightenment and void,
And forgetting the hard times.
I'm a Queen without a King,
Living in a palace and not cage.
Living in luxury gave me pain,
But leaving luxury gave me peace.
I fought all the way,
To search my own way.
Do not mistake my silence,
For my weakness.
I surrendered, to let you live a life.
and to give myself the best life,
chirping and singing my own song,
The thing that I deserved since so long.

Home

Sunshine glimmers
Through cranny windows.
The wood smells like,
Burnt cocoa.
Reminiscent of the childhood
That's sweet to cherish,
Yet dubious and bygone.
That's how unreal it feels.

The bamboo wind chime
Still rests and swings
With the flow of the breeze
Just like my life
That rippled me,
To where I am today.

The chimes remain
Consistent over the years.
What changed, was my life
With every beat it produced.

The wax carvings on walls
Which are rather deeply etched
On my heart
As precious as Picasso's art.
The sheer and pale curtains

Were a sign of arrival of comfort
As its texture carried
The warmth of mother's palms.

The chest of drawers
In the corner of the room
Was indeed rich of memories,
Albums and archaic jewellery.

Till this day,
I hear the giggles
In the wind circulation
Inside the house.

Once it was my haven,
And now,
Being here once again,
It feels like
This is how heaven must be.

Gratification

Sometimes it is okay
To grow weary of a leisure pursuit.
Isn't it a symbol,
Of your undying love for it?
You dissolved yourself totally in it.
That it left you exhausted,
Isn't it a part,
Of your partial victory?
You already tasted
The gratification from it.

Tales

The photo frames,
Hanging on the walls
Are windows
To so many tales.
That are exquisite.
Every time you look at them,
It takes you to a different land.
That's inexistent.
But it feels good,
To stay wherever it is.

Too much of it

They ridiculed my fatty flabs,
My robust built
And my thighs,
Fighting for space or "gap".
Once,
It was unbearable
To take so much in
Maybe because I thought
I already had "too much" in me.
Too much of skin?
Too much of shame?
Too much of nerve to exist?
But once
I thought of letting it all go
For "once",
And no matter what taunts and jokes
They came up with next time,
The very next moment,
I was loving my body all over again.

Phoenix

I like to be called a phoenix
It makes me feel fecund
Capable of producing so much strength
From nearly dead roots.
That my ashes hide the spark to provocate into fire.
When I'm looked upon as a speck of dust,
But my existence revelates to the viewer.
My two-fold wings
Are that of fire and passion.
I sprinkle my skin on the land that I stand.
To reward the ones who have passion melting in them.
After shedding the past me,
Into my burning aura
I do not blame the person I was.
Because I arose from my own predecessor.
And I cannot be more thankful to myself for birthing me
into a new, evolved free bird.
My wings fanned the flames to burn myself,
It was a test of my endurance,
Because no diamond becomes one,
Without the heat inflicted by the fire.

Sakura

Sakura, Oh Sakura
What cherished elixirs of souvenir you have in save.
For us to savour
Until our tongues turn pink and
Veins colour crimson.

Your cascade of overwhelming sighs,
Fall piece by piece;
Onto the faithful rivers of goodbyes.
The devotees part and hearts ache.

Your trunk is a shrine
For I bow-down at your roots
To let me feel once more
The beauty to row boats with oars

As I stream down the fuchsia river,
With all your gifts full in my palms.
All I ask you is to gift me more memories
Full in my heart.

For now, I go
To see you blossom once more
You bore no cherries,
But I'll return back for more and merry.

Childhood

Round and round,
Goes merry-go-round.
She steps up on it,
Like a queen's pedestal.
Mulled over the times,
Her hands glistened.
With magical dust,
Of crushed conch shells.
Her throne lied,
On a plate of rainbow.
Going round over like
A time-machine drawing,
Her back to the carefree times.

Fairy Myself

I tip toe through the rainforest
In the puddles like raindrops.
Caressing every tree in my way
I reach the core where canopies
home me.
And the barks grow crystals
From my icy touch.
Their shine dissolves into my face
And I love each reflection of my flaws softly.
I consider the crystals,
A concealed me.
Enlightened by the aura of pure serenity.
The petrichor slumbers in the blanket of air
Prompting me the power of persuading
Dragons of wildfires into believing
They are Unicorns kissing my forehead.
As they nuzzle some self-love out in me.
They wave the horn at me in vow
And I leave for diving down the streams.
Gulping litres of Water and not afraid of choking.
Tell the man on the watercraft to change its ways.
And the waves roll underneath and do as I say.
For I no more need the leap of reassurance.
I traverse to the riverbanks.
Like water like drapes.
I'm no boat but I cut through in a sheath.

The moist moss coral reefs
Render memories of many that soaked
The goodness in.
They say this forest emits rich legacy,
That any being becomes porous,
And self-love fills their lungs
Like air that's born on the first day.
And the hearts feel new like dew doused leaves.

Mindfulness

I've tasted buildings,
Like the coffee comfort.
The warmth of apartments,
I've never been to.
The melting decor,
Of yellow chandeliers.
Touch softly my heart.
Like piercing hot cocoa.
This is a kind of high.
I wanna keep daydreaming about.
When the days are colored blue.
And they pour pure rains.
The window sills,
Stay petrichor.
From the honey touch
Of the drops that shower love.
What's so special about this?
It's a day I gift myself,
To walk around and see.
Admire the beauty and breathe.

Naïve Kid

A naive kid was savoured in an uncooked meal
With all her flavours naturally enticing
The taste buds of her forefathers,
As she frolicked around the unblemished skies.
For kids were always
Meant to be naive.
Yet with the Theory of Evolution
Charles Darwin advanced a question mark
On all the rawness of a callow sapling.
Her ancestors always loved the blank canvas
She was.
Because she was pristine yet fulfilling
Helping them run their inner artist wild.
But,
The flames of this world
Have barbequed the innocence out of her.
She wasn't the one to be melt in a mould in a world that called her gullible.
Because homo sapiens nowadays,
like their food smoked.

Natural

Every rose has its thorns,
And same way even
I have flaws.
And if you want
To store my scent.
Then take me naturally,
As I am.

Kintsugi

Some hearts break ruthlessly
But they mend with
Beauty and power.
They might not stay
Perfect as they were.
But imperfections become
Their perfect embellishments.

Heart Home

And a day will come,
When you'll find.
The crumbled pieces,
Of your beautiful heart.
Carefully rebuilding,
Into a castle of hope.
Where you will
Find yourself
Comfortable in it
Once again.

Helium Bar

All around the jokers dance,
Banger music chokes the crowd.
Finally risking all my life,
Gulping spit and loosing ties.
Gassed up balloons tied around their heads,
Floating up on helium flavoured air.
Blanched cups clink,
From our exchanged breath
Mystifying our sudden misty future.
All I say,
Is the helium language.
My words hang upside down over your head space.
Maybe because I'm in a dizzy state.
Hold the warmth I put in them,
Before they rise above your name.
The boat openings in my eyes,
See through the bright blue light.
Acting like a siren,
In the deep blue sea.
Sing me a lullaby addicting to the ears.
Like our ancient trend of lies.
I know I'm drowning,
And the boats are seeping highs.
But this time the surrounding water
Is the one of ease,
And one that could keep me grounded

Yet not on my knees,

Or leaving me crave for the actual life.

I'm learning to accept my emotions

Emotional Psyche

Hear me out, I'm in pain
Not physical, but mental.
Clenched fists with recurrent fits
A symptom that's clinical,
Apparently more mythical.

In a society which carries,
Stereotypical people.
Who's going to step forward, and
Break the folk of folks, to whom
It's merely, just a hoax.

Stop denying the need for help,
Because it might be need of the hour.
To a sufferer who dwelt, days sucked,
In a whirlpool.

A whirlpool of Whims, and bewilderment.
People who turn their backs, and act all skeptical.
I'm tired of being shunned and shut,
said the inner voice lamenting.

Let's unify and let them uncover,
The true self,
By seeking mental help,
For maintaining mental health.

Odd

A place which seems, different than my abstract
All covered in gloss of humanity.
Underneath lies, the delusional mankind.
A community where, civilization speaks
The language of, shame and sin.
A paradise which smells fusty and rusty,
Such irony at its peak.
The era of new generation,
With different outlook,
Towards the reality of psychological well-being.
Sadly, holds a pedestal only in fantasy.
Shame is the interpretation of mental health
An unending spiral of spicy gossips,
Because none is ready to beat all odds
And become an odd one.

Passenger

A road that turns, two ways,
A choice to take, anyone.
Either way, the wanderer takes,
Will lead him on the run,
And remould him to a passenger,
A passenger of purpose and desire.
Some travel to holy shrines and wash away
All sins.
Some travel miles just to meet their kins.
Some travel to admire the aesthetic engraves,
Others just to dive into the history of native caves.
Some go to bond with the souls of
Different lands.
Others just to taste cultures hand in hand.
Some travel through the gates of architecture,
While others through their own mind's mirror.

Rebirth

I suddenly woke up,
Just to find myself up
In a deep, dark and gloomy place.
It should rather be called a pit
A pitch-black pit.

It hurts my head,
To think of arising from it.
It's like a tragedy has befallen on me,
And made me fall into it.

All I hear are the crickets,
Becoming a part of my isolation.
And not a single soul to pick me up,
From my own grave of hallucinations.

It feels like a haven,
But I know it's not.
I try so hard to pull myself out,
Out of the misery, I'm somehow stuck in.
Just like a bee in its own beeswax.

My stinger is stinging my own body,
I'd leave only after, my own destruction.
I have lost the ability to dig
What's wrong and what's not.

I've lost the shovel,
I used to dig my own pit with.
You can't help me
With the same shovel,
As you'll try to fill,
The void in me
You'll bury me alive,
Because you think I'm dead.

I'm the ash
That can still,
Transform into fire.
All I need is your little help.
Just some air, to make me spark.

I promise I'd be the fire,
To engulf negativity.
But never diminish,
My own blaze.

Burning so hot,
I'd never think of a drop of water
I'll know what I'm worth,
And I'll be the phoenix
Who, from its own ashes,
Takes rebirth.

Hidden

These winters make me,
Come undone.
To my not so beautiful past.
It unburdens the baggage,
Like pines shedding snow.
Crowds drown me,
And the rusted leaves bury the body.
Shadows walk past the tomb
And some create a stampede.
All that's left,
Is now the gunpowder of leaves,
Waiting to be set on a wildfire.

Dry Life

Those eyes feel dry
Can't even cry
All there's left inside
Is a prickly comfort.
The world is at a sudden halt,
The sculpture looks
Oddly a human
Begging to be thawed.
The mist on the leaves
Weighs them down.
That tree is a crib
To most of its pain.
No matter how
A person tries to find warmth
All there's left
Is our porous heart
Combating cold.

Regret or Avoid?

Regret is like a missed train,
The pleasure of reaching the destination,
For the purpose could have been
From sanders to sandalwood.
Mellow and breezy.

Avoiding is like an availed flight,
The pleasure of rushing adrenaline,
For the present could have been
An avoided yet availed chance to fly away.

It's the beauty of avoiding some things,
Probably the most notorious word
We have ever come across.

But isn't it finer to avoid,
Instead of regret?
Because some things,
Leave you lifeless
The more you forge towards them.

Why don't we see avoiding,
As a golden chance
That knocks on your door,
On rare occasions?

Maybe,
avoiding a thunderous moonlight
Is better,
than regretting a lifeless night.

She's on Fire

Note-: Gaslighting is a form of manipulation by a loved one or close person into making a person believe that they are insane or aren't thinking straight for whatever situation.

Left, right, left, left
Right, right, left..
What route to take next?
All the walls look the same.

Somehow the colour
Looks all black
The bricks textured
Whispers of him.

I only see
Crooked paths
And every left
Appears to be right
But every right is always left.

I walked on stars
to reach the moon
Not knowing
It'd prick like broken glasses.

I left the entrance 5 minutes back
But here I meet it again
Was it the exit I entered?
Or is this all an illusion.

Am I under the spell of delusions?
Or is this a giant hoax.
My eyes hurt
Looking straight at the bright beam.

As I was about to reach the end
It distracted me
Like the light
Used to scare away wild boars.

I'm stuck in a maze
This game is a loved one's creation
He said, he will get me.
But I wonder when.
Is it me who can't see?
Him around me
Or is it him
Wearing the cloak of bright lights.
I guess I'll never know
Where he is,
Or if he is or not.
Because my eyes have become
As dark as a black hole

Vacuuming all the reality
To the state of void.

Voice crack

My voice cracked,
As if
All the wounds were,
Oozing the pain out,
Between the silences of the cracks.

My confidence,
Was melting,
Like hot lava from a volcano.
And no one dares to put water on the heat.
Its steam is quite dangerous.
It engulfs the one who saves me.

My courage,
Was breaking,
Slowly into the foundation,
From which once it arose.
Piece by piece,
My hard made castle,
Was demolishing itself.

My world came down shattering,
The glasses were shaking
And ringing,
As if the arrival of a storm
But who's going to tell me.

That it has already,
Gone to where it started.
I'm back to square one.

Circus World

I'll laugh
Till the inch of the ring extends
I'll laugh
Till mine is in sync with theirs.
I'll laugh
Till my conscience hits me with a brick.

I cursed my soul
For being disloyal to the body
And blending into the crowd
To ridicule me.
Of course, it isn't accountable to anybody.
It changes its company in every lifetime.

I'll laugh
Till the inch of the ring extends
I'll laugh
Till mine is in sync with theirs.
I'll laugh
Till my conscience hits me with a brick.

A monkey dances
Until the spectators
Go rolling on the floor
With their bellies hurting.

That ring becomes
A test of its skills
That ring becomes
A border of war front.

I'll laugh
Till the inch of the ring extends
I'll laugh
Till mine is in sync with theirs.
I'll laugh
Till my conscience hits me with a brick.

The monkey keeps on dancing,
It keeps on juggling
To let its conscience save him
Or to let the spectator's feed
On the show he puts on.

What to do
Or what not to.
He loses his consciousness
In a feast
That's fun not for him but for all.
He spins into a cartwheel
Shuffling all his insides.
Increasing the dizziness
With a taste of anaesthesia on his tongue.

Body moves but the gaze is fixed,
On that giant, fancy entrance of the tent.
Which might stand upright
Only as an entry for him.

He'd be out when,
His soul waves at him mockingly,
Tailoring the next body
It wants to make home in.

It will laugh,
Till the coward cloak lives.
It will laugh
Till it smells pain.
It will laugh
Till it zips a costume on him.

Mental Illness

Mental illness makes us go back
To where we started.
Our pace suddenly decreases.
We feel like the world is going forward
While there's some weird vacuum
Sucking us back to some lonely
Black hole.

It feels like a train moving backwards,
And an illusion of inversion.
But it's tough
To make your heart understand,
That what's different is only the pace.
We might feel like we aren't able to
Keep up with the world at the same speed
But we are moving, too.

We are moving towards our goals,
Success and happiness, too.
Our paths maybe different
But some-how they are same.
As we both move.
It's the law of this universe,
Nothing stops.
Not even thoughts,
Not even galaxies.

Not even planets
And not even stars.

We might feel like a snail,
Paving its way home.
But that little creature with load
On his back,
Would reach a safe space, too.

Then how could we believe,
The false fact that we are still.

Held hands and cried

Grief and sorrow are mutual friends
To many of us out there.
It's because when ocean floor
Loses its control over the stirred-up emotions.
Its waves go high and low,
Like its energy has been bottled up into a
Secured show.
The high tides,
Soak up the salty breeze
Into the sole of the low spirits
Of a miserable soul.
And it washes away the intangible cloth
That makes up the inside.
And finally, the blues fall from the eyes.
Rhythmic sobs into the beats of Oceanic waves.
The colourless tears,
Reflect the faces of many that broke
Into the same ocean of cries.
And this is how we all hold
Hands with melancholic sighs.

Love Lone

Love lone is the new kind of loneliness from love.

I couldn't find one accurate enough on google to describe this feeling that a lot of us are going through.

It feels like nobody is willing to walk an extra mile for you. You're in a garden full of roses yet nobody comes to pluck you one. You pluck one for yourself, but it wilts quite fast from the loneliness that soaks into its petals. Loneliness is rather communicable. It engulfs everyone around you, and that again makes you lonelier and love lone. You mourn in the deep, dark night of a far-off forest, but this daylight sucks even your shadow away from you.

You binge eat and embed your feelings under the blanket of food cravings. But the mean comments to your weight gain ask you to shed the fat shavings. Your too big body pushed everyone away, your too small body choked you for breath. Your heart always cribs for emotional warmth and support, but they end up demeaning you of a creeper and parasite needy of support.

You hope for days full of sunshine and night full of moonlight, but when you're lone, not even the sun shows up his face and not even the moon turns up to your gate.

You look for ways to shove your face into your pillow, because good company now no more lures you. It keeps you in bed until someone forces you to get some fresh air. You think it’s just loneliness and it will be gone one day, but that day never comes because you are surrounded by so many other conditions to face. Your self-esteem loves to stay in your roots, when you're working so hard to pull it up to your height at least. You keep looking for perfect fairy tales ending on good days, but the prince charming never comes on his white horse tying your shoe lace or plant a warm kiss on your face.

Gloom: Another Episode

My palms reined life,
To halt the painful eves.
Mashed a citrus marmalade,
Existential jelly.
Scooped and tossed
One into that mouth
Drooling with honey.
Shoved the face in pillow,
And travelled in search of
Unfinished tears.
When found one
They said we deal in business
Of scraping fears.
And laying out dishes made of salt.
Crispy and brittle.
Just as your heart you prepared out,
To be cold and fragile to see.
The edges of short boundary walls,
Entice to skip them over.
But the rails inside mind,
Too tall to overstep.
So, they stood,
At the edge of the sparks.
Danced from one to another.
Until they skipped a step.
And fell for their end.

A start of something pristine.
Was yet to begin.
They hope to pounce
On tamarind healthy times,
Shade of palms that bore coconut
And seems ripe.
They want to ride
With the cream,
And silk-satin dreams.

Lone tapestry of Lost Friendships

Every rose on her garland
Was like walking on a bed
With buttered sole.
But the ivies
Slept poised from dusk to dawn.
With a veiled lisle
Tying them to their inaugural
Snippet of its friendships.

So, the girl with roses,
Wandered around on thorns
On her crown.
In search of,
A disguised drop of love rings.
Made of thin threads, probably lisles.
Her idea of luxury was,
Love rooting from the pricks of the flowers
Growing beneath her heels.

After endeavouring falls
From sky-high
And quivers
Running down her thighs.
She was made into believing
That some do not amass empires
Embellished threads of poised ivies.

And that realisation
With a deep breath
Barely seeping into her chest
Hit the bodies of salinity
Spinning into the dead sea.

Her body choked
In the crowd of ivies.
The name never leaves.
And she settled afloat,
Even water therapy
Couldn't rinse the weight off her body.
And she settled afloat
From the cloak on skin
But the mind therein
Drowned way before.
Piercing through the needles
Poisoned of anxiety,
Infecting her forever.

Anxiety: Eyes on Me

At a distance
My past disguises in future
It pulls me into a magnetic field.
It sits far off on an arena bench
But feels too close like a brush on my skin.
The corners all blend in a circle of dry leaves
Burnt till the trail reaches me.
It shrinks like a cotton rag.
Suffocating me inside.
The fabric of utmost ventilation
Makes me gasp for air as if claustrophobic space.
My heavy eyes hold back wild tears,
With reigns of reassurance.
Until they no more can
And burst open into an open field of isolation.
Isolation that comes with pre-requisites prescribed on my mind.
That company comes to those who crib less.
Who's going to tell me, that it's an endless whirlpool I've entered in.
It's a place I've been to before, then how does it get tough when I reach back again?
Someone who could cover me the span between habits and jamais vu.

What is This?

I was rolling over good times,
When suddenly,
A ruthless force flickered in my stomach.
The feeling of falling from heights.
But I'm grounded in my place.
I choke on dry ice.
My palms were forced to feel the pricking needles.
I was dizzy in a parallel universe.
Light headed and dashing in and out.
I'm happy in the party of life
But I'm also shivering in the cold night skies.
I'm alone in my attic,
Still see shadows walk past by.
The windows puke spotlight,
As if all folks were desperate to see my outline.
A nomad drifted through a heap of dry leaves.
By the wind that gushes and releases
Its tasteless fearsome life on me.
And my body sinks into my bed.
As my eyes try to find solace
In the dark of a duvet.
Will you switch the table lamp on?
After all attempts failed,
I don't know what this is.
Maybe light closer will lure me
To fly like fireflies.

Solace After

It has come.
It has all come over me.
I've been forced to jell under a rock.
It's too heavy on me.
My eyes are swelling from tears.
They are oozing out constant pain
But no one,
Absolutely no one see the water
Absorbed in the soil beneath me.
I'm kicking my feet in thin air.
It knows the excruciating pain
Inside me.
Yet it chooses to ignore me.
I wish the force kills me.
But all that it leaves me with
Are blood clots stretching my skin.
I wish to end this all,
But they will make
A home under the rock
And crave my presence.
I'll be far off the shore,
When they'll start anew of depression.
I could leave a bottled letter behind,
But my wrist already pains
From the words that are designed.
Please don't see me

As I fade away in your sleep.
I hope your days aren't lonely
As I'm forgotten
Like no part of me ever existed.
And the solace might find me,
When I retire back to my sheets.

I'm also like you

Crimson Dawn

Is it that time of the month,
Defines her mood.
She was genuinely sad,
And not rude.
Such pure is the stain,
A symbol of life.
She bears intense pain,
A smile is enough to hide.
She keeps a track of every date,
Try for once to make her feel great.
The society cares enough,
To vanish all pickles.
But forget the same palms,
That made it taste so flavourful.
They tell her to forbid,
Stepping into the temple.
Ignoring the goddess,
They worship for rituals.
God's creation became,
A dark and gloomy secret.
The day her cycle starts,
She moves back to her attic.
They kept this wealth,
with utmost stealth.
For her it became an everlasting spell,
When she couldn't actually,

Stay, “Stayfree”.
With hope in her head,
And isolation around her bed.
Every next cycle to come,
She dreads.
We have evolved from cotton rags,
To tampons and knitted pads.
How much more time?
To unravel the shackles,
Of stereotypical minds.
For her to loosen,
Her sweaty fists and knuckles.
Even a pad is capable,
Of absorbing the crux of life.
When will the world be ready,
To absorb the state of what she goes through.
The same world that she gave,
Birth to.

<u>She</u>

A life, pea sized
Yet it carries, the entire cosmos
In its sparkling eyes.
Her skin as delicate, as rose.

Her sapphire eyes,
That carry,
The richness of the oceans.
The rage of the coasts
And the calm of the waves.

Her shoulders so strong,
That carry the thick wings.
Her head held high,
As she soars into the sky.

Her crown so light,
Emits halo light
Of reigning the nature,
An angelic gesture.

Her hair chestnut brown,
Fertile as soil.
The base of every mountain
And a source to extract oil.
Her feet rooted to the ground,

As the river flows,
Through the gaps of her fingers
And turn so pure.

Her arms always open,
To welcome all lives.
As they enter,
Through the gates of heavenly skies.

Kins

As I entered
The doors,
Of my close kins.
My ears absorbed,
A careless,
And an apathetic
Response,
To my outlook.
And I knew,
What it was going to be.
They used to cover their apathy,
In a disguise of concern.
Just like long distances,
It took us long enough, and so many days
To meet them again.
Yet,
They preferred to pierce my ears
Through needles that felt painful.
I know I've gained,
Another robe of skin over skin,
But for once,
Let's just celebrate over souls,
And not just the cloaks.
Let's cherish the meet after parting.
For ages our spirits have endured.
I expect a little space in your hearts,

Not,

Because I'm big

But,

Because I want to know,

How it feels to live in a place,

Bigger than me.

I cut my Hair

It's bothersome
To listen to people
Asking me ritually,
As to why I cut my hair so short
It's like they worship my hair long
And devote less when they're short.
I answer exhaustedly
It's because of all the conversations
That play in my head and continuously
Play on my long hair.
I had to get them off their play zone.
It's because of the smell
Of all the unwanted memories
In them.
I wanted to bleach them away
From the surface of my hair.
It's because of the gloom
Coloured touch you left in the locks
Of my hair.
It's because of all the broken promises
That pierced like blade all the way through to my hair.
That I feel free with short hair.
It's because I wanted
To get rid of all the burden
Of our so-called emotions we shared
That were built up on my hair.

Goldflower

You see an ornament,
Dripping from your lover's neck.
He comes your way
And that piece dangles all the way back from a galaxy,
To the one that shines in your eyes.
He is too unstable to adjust his eyes on your face.
I won't say further,
Now you know what sorcery,
That jewellery piece relays.
As his mouth vomits dollars
With frail face bewitched.

Facing Herself

The crest of my blazer
Is crisp and crystallized
Ready to fall off any minute.

Ask the broken compass in it,
The needles waver north to south
Like my thighs that quiver
At the sight of his eyes.

Running my hands
Through the edgy leaves,
As the presence of knives never leave
He pays me, in pennies and grands.

Will a serving help the woman run her day?
Or would the matted hair rescue her away.
Ask his muted fists,
Ready to staple her locks, Oh Christ.

It's a new day
As she rolls over crimson cushions
One on waist, two on thighs
Three on face and the soaked cries.

She hides away like masquerade,
Pretending to be in game.

While he opens the door wide,
She whispers to her genitalia
You are strong, you'll get through
Without a loud sigh.

And once we're done,
Maybe then you will survive.
He goes away slamming the jammed door.
And her throat feels stuffed,
From the agony build up.

Full coverage foundation,
Off she goes to store.
Oh, I'm allergic to sun,
So, an automated receipt,
Releases from the vendor's mouth
I asked for none,
Was a sentence written by.

The curtains drop,
As the sobs turn to hush.
And the lady in blazer,
Nervously adjusts her dress.
As the narrator ends the play.

Childhood- part-2 (reimagined)

Round and round
Goes merry-go-round.
She steps up on it,
Like a Queen.
Only to find,
A plate of rainbow
Drawing her back,
To the spring and limes.
Oblivious of,
The broken pedestal of society.
That took her to a surprising era of time.
Where monochromes couldn't welcome,
People wrapped in flags of spectrum
Bringing themselves hues of joy.
When monos themselves giggled,
On the same plate of rainbow
In some other time-frame.

Estranged

They say she is,
Estranged wealth.
But her love for them,
Was unconditional.
They build her up,
With utmost stealth
Because these obligations
Are meant to be traditional.
Sometimes I think,
Out of the blue.
What if all this,
Comes to be true.
Will they forget,
Their little princess.
As she descends the house,
And they bless.

Human

I will show my emotions,
But will hide my feelings.
I will show stone heart,
But will feel from heart.
I will be confident,
But stay fragile.
I will give deaf ears,
But listen carefully.
I will forgive easily,
But never forget easily.
I will uncover fake smile,
But will cover happiness.
I will be vulnerable,
But keep myself secure.
I will hide my humanity,
But will I still be a human?

I love you

Wine of Love

Strolling around the artsy town,
Of crooked lanes and cobblestones.
Every stone is a milestone,
Of Love, or of Hate,
Of Guilt, or of Fate.
Wearing a tuxedo, just Unceremonious,
A symbol of splendour, nearly odd.
I'm a peddler of hearts,
Stuck on one.
That one belongs to you.
Let's sit under the shade of Boho canopy,
And sip a glass, each of Riesling from 1850.
Know the passion, I have for you,
In every sip of holy wine.
Love is the gift from divine itself,
Wine is the way to spellbound Love.
If you leave the setting anyway,
I'll wait for the day,
My feelings will perish.
Over time, they might wear out,
But remember that, one day
They will revive again.
When I'll drink the same Riesling from 1850,
And I will drown myself,
In the Wine of Love,
All over again.

Epiphany

A flower orchard, so vivid
Like a palette of all shades
Some bright and some pastel
While some grey, others blue.
Single wilted flower, much blue and grey
In a meadow, of blooming flowers
The wind came gushing,
Mistaking the wilted flowers,
To be bowing in honour.
It strokes the wilted petals,
Being lured by its probity.
Unknown of its pain,
That made it escape to vain.
That touch proved to be magical,
So alive to the petals,
And the flower bloomed again
In epiphany of being alive,
And in love.
The wind stopped by,
For a minute.
As if life, came to halt.
Everything felt so alive, even at stop.
As if kept in a perfect frame,
To be admired and to stay,
Forever the same.
Time moved on,

When reality swayed again.
The flower then realised,
How a sudden euphoria,
Brought it back to life.
How beautiful is the love of wind for flowers.
It makes them feel alive,
But also makes them withstand
It's pure rage
As a tornado hits by.
Without a complain,
They stand there blooming.
In wait of wind.
As it blows again.

One whom you expect

It was midnight
Pitch black outside (rain in the background)
And in my head
Monochrome.

A thought struck at 12:01
Why are so many hearts broken?
When we have so many hearts,
Broken.

Hasn't there been anything,
To tape hearts,
Like nothing ever,
And forever.

Another struck at 12:02
Why do people write their feelings
At places they are anonymous?
In the hope of being understood by some
Stranger out there.

But why do we expect something from,
People behind screens
And not from people
Who could actually make us free.
That one person never comes

As we want them to understand us,
Love us, reach us,
They never do.

Another struck at 12:04
Why do we sit idle,
Listening to songs
On loop?

When we can listen to beautiful melodies,
People have out there.
Maybe because they are too busy,
Keeping their music anonymous.
At the end, they never come,
When we want them to open up to us.

Another struck at 12:05
Why don't they listen to our melody?
Is it because it isn't audible.
Or because they chose not to listen.

We sure have beautiful hearts,
But they chose not to see the beauty in it.
Maybe because then this world won't be a
Rich place to live in.

As every story ends,
They never come,

And never listen
To what magic our hearts hold.

Nights pass by,
Just like this
Wandering in my own thoughts
Asking a question, every minute.
But they never come,
To answer any.

Parallel Universe

As I depart to my bed
And fall into the arms,
Of deep sleep.
My mind makes me believe
Maybe there exists, a parallel universe
To live, and to see.

And if it does, I feel
Another 'You', exists too
Probably laying close beside me.

Fragments of our skin will brush and fall off,
They will turn to fireflies and unite us,
By lighting up our future ahead.

The butterfly that sat on your skin
Will touch my lips and drip
Its nectar making me feel
Warm, as if your kiss.

The night we held hands, under the vast
Stretches of universe felt as if an
Unending blanket, an impenetrable
Armor to my fragile heart and keep us cosy.

The lavenders will bloom perfuming the aura,

Soothing our souls.
Roses will wilt,
In the honour of our love.

The bees will play the angel,
Sucking nectar from honeysuckle
Leaving us honey to drink.
A warm tonic to nourish,
Before a good night's sleep.

As I sail to the 5th stage of my sleep,
I fear of not finding you beside me.
After all, they say, love so beautiful.
Happens only in dreams.

Moon

Woke up in the middle of the night
To open myself up, at the end
Through the hands of a glowing ball,
My porcelain like friend.
Without giving a call,
I meet every night.

It shows me its craters
I show it my wounds
We share a bond indifferent,
From the earthers.

They say it smells
Burnt ashes and smoke.
I sense its foggy mist,
Pacify my soul.

It offers to sing me a lullaby,
The nights calm
So, I sleep peacefully,
In its arms.

They are scared of its haunting visit,
It pays every night.
I wait for the white lilies to bloom,
And smile at its sight.

My dearest friend saves me,
In the darkest of nights,
In the thickest of forests.
It finds me when I'm struggling
To hide myself into the void.

For once, my friend,
I want to be there for you.
When you hide yourself,
Into the daylight.

Veiled

We look at that one person from the corner of our eyes because we do not have the guts to even face them. We know, that person can never be ours. That excruciating pain that hits our heart like a sword pierced through it, letting warm blood flow all over our bodies. It feels comforting yet uneasy. Why? Is it because of love and separation or loneliness and void that we are constantly trying to fill? But we try all over again and it never really happens. Gathering false hopes with every dawn to dusk and then laying on the floor of our room with scattered hope every night. This whirlpool never stops, rather it tosses and flings our souls out of our body, leaving us unconscious about our surroundings, and sucks us all the way deep into the eye of darkness.

How blue and black?

The top feels too distant to reach, as if the crown of a skyscraper. It feels like we are a part of the concealed attic in the building. It's always overlooked and no one ever tried to look behind that veil.

We always hid and blended into the background, waiting for the special someone to find us back to our senses and reality. We wait and wait and always wait. Our soul shatters everyday into the resilient waves of the ocean. It is never too weak to be broken by us, but always too raging to strip us from skin to bone. The blood dissolves deep into the blue ocean and we still look for the lighthouse that never appears. Is it love that's keeping me going or loneliness telling me to stop and give up?

Breeze and Blunt

Your eyes hold paintings in them.
They're as blue as a deep ocean,
I see so many stories.
Some of rocky pasts
And others of serene beauty.
Beauty of the countless rendezvous.
With bosom buddies and tied bloodline.
Flowing into the rivers of matured Wine.
Old and therapeutic thyme.
I wish to thank your old master, unfeigned.
For coming up with such a hue.
Of blues and cools.
The one that's found at Aurora Polaris.
It's the show of a lifetime,
I see in your eyes.
The upbeat lights of jolly delights,
The slow ones of the sombre times.

Unrequited

I liked the feeling,
When you passed by me.
Your perfumed feather
Lifted me into a heaven,
I thought existed.

It felt light,
As the breeze,
Brushed the tip of my nose,
And I mistook it, for love was in the air.

The pink wasn't around me,
But in my mind.
For I got fooled,
By a sudden blood-rush in my cheeks.

My heart beat fast,

But swiftly it dropped,
From the tower of expectations.
Because you,
Weren't really into me.
The jacket felt warm,
For I felt secured.
Insecure was my heart
In your delusional embrace.

My heart broke,
Many times
But you couldn't hear it crush.
For your ears were buried,
Deep in my chest for help.
And eyes building up tears
From sobs to hush.

My eyes cried so much,
That the tears came out velvety.
The cheeks textured rumple,
As a worn fabric.

I loved you so much,
And I couldn't be more direct.
I wanted you to love me,
Just the way I wished you would.

Charms

The blazing shine it emits
From far away.
They wear these charms
All over the body.

Is it the tarnished beauty,
Or the revealed shine?
This unseen force of its charms
Attracts my soul to him.

But how will my soul distinguish,
The coat on his heart?
The one of oxidized simplicity
Or the one with lustrous felicity.

What if the lacklustre eyes,
Hold the proficiency to be my muse?
What if his sparkling cloak,
Wraps a meaningless hollow?

I stare into the void,
As he walks around me
Encased in full glory.
I'd wish a grounded someone,
Than a prideful conqueror.

At the end,
I didn't let my psyche,
Entice me
With all the charms in his pocket.

Tough Love

Your heart is as cold as winters
A passionate kiss could melt your cold
Heart and it would feel like drowning
Into the water of sudden ease.

Your breath felt stale and dried up,
Why don't you tell me what caged you?
In your own shackles.

I would've pierced through, just for you.
Burning like an iron baton,
Straight out of a blazing furnace.
My heat might feel intensely pricking.
But the enchanting burn would,
Always be etched on your heart.

Love Booze

It's the tropical night
Alone on an island
With you by my side
Your hands are in mine

My heart is gassed up
Like an intoxicated bottle of champagne.
I can't hold it in anymore
It might explode with butterflies.

The neon lights,
Under the wood shack
Keep flickering
Like my eyes looking at you.

All I see
Is me dancing
Under the canopy of stars
In the blackberry sky.

The euphoric rush
In my veins
Lights some spark in me
Like fireworks in the sky.
I like our tangy bond
Full of salty breeze

Sweet and sour talks
And candid memories.

I swim through silky drinks
To the sky
I taste the candied moon
When I'm with you.

It's the cupid,
Who creates dizzy drinks.
Makes us drown
In the elixir of emotions
Made with love.

You're my little boo
And I'm in Love booze.
I'm drunk on mint honey dew
You take away all my blue lagoons.

Between the Spaces

Do you stand under the vast sky?
And think of sharing it with me.
Or do the shooting stars
Make you wish for me?

Do you think of all the butterflies?
That ever collided with your skin
And doused you in my kisses.
That I sent while you were away.

Do you run distances
To cover the space between us
Or will we lay close
Even through the map of telephone lines.

Do you sip coffee,
Reminiscing the memories, we made.
Or the khaki froth,
Emanates the warmth of our hugs.

Do you connect with me?
Like the non-existent corners of a circle.
Or the cycle you ride
Would be a sign for you to return back to me.
Do you dream,
Like it was yesterday?

And that's the only way for me,
To slip into your life again.

Whatever may be the distance between us,
I believe it's meant to be,
In all the other lifetimes.
As long as it is to spend with you, I'm yours alone.

Telekinesis

I saw a boy,
Walking down the alley
He was tall and brown-eyed
Chestnut hair and riding a bike.

His go to café
Was the Pot of warmth.
An old lady's haven
And his one and only heaven.

The day I saw him,
Was the day my heart skipped a beat
I thought that's strange,
Because how can a man make it possible
Without having to talk to me.

But the café owner,
Was a psychic lady.
She had the abilities none possessed.
Her coffee had the warmth
Even with the undone cocoa zest.

Her every drop of cocoa bead
In the coffee sounded like
An enchanting plink
It lured the passer-by to have a drink

Just the way Chestnut guy did,
He fell in love with the coffee
In a blink of an eye.
Then I was just a human falling in love with another.

His insides used to growl,
Even at the whiff of the silky warmth of the coffee.
How easy was for the old lady,
To attract bees to the nectar.

This love doesn't have any twist,
That your heart craves for.
This is simply telekinesis,
Of love as a bewitching tool
Lifting you to a place without a single nudge.

Astrology

Flipping through aces and pentacles
While you go around playing bluff
Like the playing cards.
52 times and 52 lies.
Joke's on me
For a couplet couldn't rhyme.
I'm back on stargazing
And tracing palm lines.
For finding checkpoints
To see through signs.
It barely shows
And the oracle knows.
For the sake of dollars
She skims through her tome.
And to keep my honour
Says, "you'll soon find in him your home".
With my heart munching on crystals and clear lies,
And my hands running bare into pockets
For pennies and dimes.
I empty the void on her table
Yearning eyes looking for label.
And I never got any,
With heart heavy
Trudging feet
I inside out myself, of the tragedy.
I'm outside of the shop

Always looking in.
Finding solace around,
As I see them walking in
Throwing cakes of salaries,
Finding soulmates with batteries.

Fix this Vision

All that my eyes want is to,
See every love poem.
Like some crusty romantic novel,
Brittle to the readers' attention span.
With the narrator's vision,
Correcting all that is wrong in my intimate life.
Despite the freshly baked croissants of realism,
That I've learned to bake from themselves, the lovelorn.
Somehow the oven pukes empty at core patties.
One bite of it, and the heart desires for stuffing that melts,
On my tongue like the empires built of chocolate,
That are designed to cage lovers,
Until there's only so much heat to make this paradise cave
in.
So, I doubt my eyes on the cliché sweetmeat,
That eats me from inside for I nowhere see love in his eyes.
And sifting nooks and crannies,
I drift towards the crowded road.
Where the arc lamp blinks,
Inviting me to the optometrist.
Where apparently no one goes back vexed.
As the signboard reads, "we show what you want to see".
I do not know how to tell her,
Underneath all the wants of dressing the heart in cataracts.
It's a need for the eyes to see behind the blindfold.

The optometrist looks through the void that lives in my eyes,
And suddenly my eyes,
Twitch from the reflection of someone actually looking in them.
It's the way my eyes swallowed the solitude,
And wheeze at the sight,
Of someone trying to explore the black hole inside.
At one glance, she knew,
That these eyes are looking for what people call love,
But who would tell her that this love,
Couldn't really evolve into what they call Love.
This love stunted into a lovelorn mess.
It still sleeps where its shadows remain.
Attempting to try the glasses for short-sightedness,
But it blurs out as if to keep me in vain.
All efforts go down the drain,
As I look for the ones with hues of red.
She says it's the one that will help you see blush on his cheeks.
While I say, "does it also make others see my blues?"
She said the only way for that to be possible is,
The navy-blue shades.
While I say, "I fear of staying in shades anymore,
I fear he might not see me anyway."
Well, that's an issue.
Why don't you try the premium quality lens?
Kaleidoscopic- for a creative dreamy night,

Coloured- any way you might want to paint your own skies,
Illusionary- you see what doesn't want to be seen the way you want,
Delusional- you see what wants to be seen by you.
I deny all of it,
As I stick the memos with my vows written on it to my tongue;
And ask for a blindfold with clear shield.
Maybe the only thing to see his motives through,
And the only way my drab eyes could absorb the sunshine;
And an unforeseen wind of new love as it comes to pick the solitude
And accompany her forever.
The way she would never have to worry for a normal eyesight ever.

Poetry

You give meaning to my thoughts,
Concrete words to my messy emotions.
You're just like a poem to me,
Sometimes we rhyme together.
And other times we don't,
But that is the time,
When we both shine together,
In our own selves.

Together

I bloomed as you came,
Just like flowers do
When sun rises.

Every day you rose,
From a cold and calm night.
And burnt yourself in heat,
To make me bloom right.

Every day I withstood,
Wild and windy storms.
To deeply thank you,
For being born.

Spaces

I look up at the sky,
In night's calm.
It felt like,
I was in its arms.
I thought that stars in the sky.
Were closest to communicate,
Never knowing that,
Sky was the space between us.

I am healed with hope

Seasons of Youth

Youth is a period
Typically sought after
Spring and green

All youngsters
As fresh as buds
Energized and lush
To have their blood rush
Into cheeks with tender flush

They bring the first ray of sunshine
With blooming lilacs.
An innocent and first love-like
Emotion deeply embellished
In each of its petals
From hues to ombre.

But every rose has its thorns.
This youth isn't easy after all.
It's the time to rise and fall
With the onset of spring and fall.

The rusted leaves
That seem lifeless
crush into the soil of hope and life.
They float into thin air

Bouncy and flashy.
Until they realise the fall of the fall.

The Induced passion in the lifeless leaves
Buries into the roots of alive trees
In the hope of flowering again
In the hope to be fulfilled again
In the hope of reviving again
Which they will,
Gradually as the "autumn" passes away
Fading into the dimming sunsets.

Medicine

Sometimes the only existence,
That cares to caress me
Is the silky wind.

Its smooth texture,
Etched warm affection
On my heart
Like a cosy balm
Healing every crack.

It's like,
Healing begins at heart
So that my heart
Has enough gloss
For the ones I heal
To glide from sheeny slides.

I wish I could,
Paint the world
Happy,
From the crystal misty
Warmth of the wind.

Sea

The sea
Washed away
Your bones
To the shore.

There is salt
Drizzled over
Like a savoury
Meal enjoyed by the sea.

Still, you beg
To drown
Into its arms
That are more like
fences;
Desperate to tear you down
To a silhouette of nothingness.

Starstruck

Not cliché
What all might think.
The nights seal me in their duvet.
And keeps me stuck
To meet stars that pass by.
This heart feels safe
Even in an open sky.
And claustrophobia seeps in,
As the doors seal tight.

The present sings me a lullaby
While the past lurked around me
To settle by.
It invokes the future in few sips of riding
Through catacombs beneath my sighs.

They say shake hands with the tenses
Always,
If you don't want to drown insane.
But it's tough to let the things pass on their own.
When you know, at every moment,
You will have to take the fall
To make it right as always, all alone.

Saudade

Life feels dissociated
Like stranded on a far-off island.
Even though water surrounds
As an effort of making everything around serene.
But these winds have an uncomfortable tinch of hurry.
I feel the tears I cried years ago,
Hitting me in the circulation.
I'm stranded and no one would search for me,
But something calls me from irony of near.
It wants me to be with it.
I don't see stars where they used to be,
But they dangle over my head like pendulums
Warning me of time dripping through my fingers.
I wanna see sunsets,
Return back to sunrise.
I want to climb mountains of worthwhile
I want to go till the edge of this world
And return back alive.
But my feet sink on ground,
Like quick-sand beneath and tied.
I'll be away from my state of mind,
Away from supportive pillars of life.
I don’t know where my world lies,
Until my liberation from separation arrives.
I've been rooted-off from my saudade,
How cruel could this life be?

Please leave me with something,
As I leave my footprints behind,
On the island of my melancholia.
Because I want to stay alone,
But not lonely as I keep my world same.

Competition

We were under no obligation
To succeed or walk
Alone.
But it became a compulsion
When no. of decreasing rewards
Became a reason of
Obscure bonds.

Life

Life is like nature,
Simple as sand
Complex as rock
Beautiful as flowers
Ugly as thorns.
Lush as trees,
Barren as deserts.
Pleasurable it appears
From far away.
Painful it becomes,
Closer you survey.
Just like the heavenly,
Lilly of the valley.
Which seeks shadow,
Under the trees.
To keep itself flourishing,
For the bees.

You never Existed

Your separation came
As an uninvited guest.
And all my blues,
Became an unknown friend.
From days to months,
Months to years.
The peace to my mind,
And ultimate weapon.
To deny your existence,
As if it never happened.

I will

Even the river
Finds its course.
Through the clots
Of rigid soil.
Then I'm just a human
Finding my way
Through the darkest of days,
Like piercing light.

Reality

Poems become
Our mirrors.
When mirrors,
Distort,
Who we really are.

Hope

Light is not tangible,
but it's there.
Hope is not visible,
But it's there.
Turn on the lights,
And look for hope again.
Look how a bulb,
Fills up the dark.
Look how the ray of hope,
Fills up your heart.
You can see again
You can feel the strength
Because light
Flows in air.
And hope
Flows in your veins.

Lesson

Part of me is strong,
Part of me is broken.
Part of me cries
At every goodbye.
Part of me is thankful
That you came by.
You taught me a lesson
I never could've thought.
Your lesson became a part of me
While you,
Just a distant memory,
I have a hard time remembering.

Fire

I'm a warm place,
To your cold body.
But I'm a cold body,
In this chilly place.
Even fire burns,
Against the cold winds
To keep your hands warm.
But sadly you're
Unable to,
Revert back all.

About the Author

Thinking in Grey- Anisha Gupta

Anisha is a student of Delhi University, pursuing Bachelors in Psychology. She believes that poetry is her home, and she returns back to it in times good or bad. She has been published in a variety of online platforms facilitated by her university and on social media ventures, as well as Reliance Industries pvt. She is a mental health advocate and strongly believes in the power of therapy to change the world into a safe place for everyone to live in. Her interests include playing kalimba, watching k-dramas, and writing poetry.

Poetry became her haven, when anxiety started finding a home in her, fencing her into isolation quite literally during the onset of covid lockdown. She completed her Higher Secondary Schooling from Maharani Gayatri Devi Girls School, Jaipur.

To connect with Anisha Gupta for anything literary- visit her poetry page on Instagram- @anisha_poetry